Applying the Standards:
STEM
Grade 1

D1279407

Credits
Content Editor: Natalie Rompella
Copy Editor: Julie B. Killian

Visit *carsondellosa.com* for correlations to Common Core, state, national, and Canadian provincial standards.

Carson-Dellosa Publishing LLC
PO Box 35665
Greensboro, NC 27425 USA
carsondellosa.com

ISBN 978-1-4838-1572-5
05-106181151

Table of Contents

Introduction

STEM education is a growing force in today's classroom. Exposure to science, technology, engineering, and math is important in twenty-first century learning as it allows students to succeed in higher education as well as a variety of careers.

While it can come in many forms, STEM education is most often presented as an engaging task that asks students to solve a problem. Additionally, creativity, collaboration, communication, and critical thinking are integral to every task. STEM projects are authentic learning tasks that guide students to address a variety of science and math standards. Also, students strengthen English Language Arts skills by recording notes and written reflections throughout the process.

In this book, students are asked to complete a range of tasks with limited resources. Materials for each task are limited to common household objects. Students are guided through each task by the steps of the engineering design process to provide a framework through which students can grow their comfort level and independently complete tasks.

Use the included rubric to guide assessment of student responses and further plan any necessary remediation. Confidence in STEM tasks will help students succeed in their school years and beyond.

Student Roles

Student collaboration is an important component of STEM learning. Encourage collaboration by having students complete tasks in groups. Teach students to communicate openly, support each other, and respect the contributions of all members. Keep in mind that collaborative grouping across achievement levels can provide benefits for all students as they pool various perspectives and experiences toward a group goal.

Consider assigning formal roles to students in each group. This will simplify the collaborative tasks needed to get a project done and done well. The basic roles of group structure are as follows:

- The *captain* leads and guides other students in their roles.

- The *guide* walks the team through the steps, keeps track of time, and encourages the team to try again.

- The *materials manager* gathers, organizes, and guides the use of materials.

- The *reporter* records the team's thoughts and reports on the final project to the class.

STEM Performance Rubric

Use this rubric as a guide for assessing students' project management skills. It can also be offered to students as a tool to show your expectations and scoring. Note: Some items may not apply to each project.

4	_____	Asks or identifies comprehensive high-level questions
	_____	Makes valid, nontrivial inferences based on evidence in the text
	_____	Uses an appropriate, complete strategy to solve the problem
	_____	Skillfully justifies the solution and strategy used
	_____	Offers insightful reasoning and strong evidence of critical thinking
	_____	Collaborates with others in each stage of the process
	_____	Effectively evaluates and organizes information and outcomes
3	_____	Asks or identifies ample high-level questions
	_____	Exhibits effective imagination and creativity
	_____	Uses an appropriate but incomplete strategy to solve the problem
	_____	Justifies answer and strategy used
	_____	Offers sufficient reasoning and evidence of critical thinking
	_____	Collaborates with others in most stages of the process
	_____	Evaluates and organizes some information or outcomes
2	_____	Asks or identifies a few related questions
	_____	Exhibits little imagination and creativity
	_____	Uses an inappropriate or unclear strategy for solving the problem
	_____	Attempts to justify answers and strategy used
	_____	Demonstrates some evidence of critical thinking
	_____	Collaborates with others if prompted
	_____	Can evaluate and organize simple information and outcomes
1	_____	Is unable to ask or identify pertinent questions
	_____	Does not exhibit adequate imagination and creativity
	_____	Uses no strategy or plan for solving the problem
	_____	Does not or cannot justify answer or strategy used
	_____	Demonstrates limited or no evidence of critical thinking
	_____	Does not collaborate with others
	_____	Cannot evaluate or organize information or outcomes

Name _____

Read the task. Then, follow the steps to complete the task.

Fizzy Fun: Chemical Reactions

Create a fizzing volcano.

Materials

clay or play dough	sugar
plastic cups	vinegar
straws	water
baking powder	cups or bowls
baking soda	pipettes or spoons
flour	

Caution: Before beginning any food activity, ask families' permission and inquire about students' food allergies and religious or other restrictions.

 Ask

What do you know? What do you need to know to get started?

_____

_____

 Imagine

What could you do?

_____

_____

📝 **Plan**

Choose an idea. Draw a model.

📝 Plan

What are your steps? Use your model to guide your plan.

_____

_____

_____

🛠 Create

Follow your plan. What is working? Do you need to try something else?

_____

_____

🔄 Improve

How could you make it better?

_____

_____

💬 Communicate

How well did it work? Is the problem solved?

_____

_____

☀ Reflect

Which ingredients caused a reaction when mixed?

_____

_____

_____

Name _____

Read the task. Then, follow the steps to complete the task.

Heart Art

The paper heart shown is symmetrical—the two sides are the same when the heart is folded down the middle. Create a symmetrical paper heart.

Materials

paper
pencils

scissors

Ask

What do you know? What do you need to know to get started?

_____

_____

Imagine

What could you do?

_____

_____

Plan

Choose an idea. Draw a model.

📝 Plan

What are your steps? Use your model to guide your plan.

_____

_____

_____

🛠 Create

Follow your plan. What is working? Do you need to try something else?

_____

_____

🔄 Improve

How could you make it better?

_____

_____

💬 Communicate

How well did it work? Is the problem solved?

_____

_____

☀ Reflect

What are some tips you would give others on how to create a symmetrical image?

_____

_____

_____

   © Carson-Dellosa · CD-104852 · Applying the Standards: STEM

Name _____

Read the task. Then, follow the steps to complete the task.

Attack of the Four-Foot Teddy Bear: Light and Shadow

Create a four-foot (1.2 m) -tall shadow of a teddy bear.

Materials

ruler, meterstick, or measuring tape

small teddy bear
flashlight

Ask

What do you know? What do you need to know to get started?

_____

_____

Imagine

What could you do?

_____

_____

Plan

Choose an idea. Draw a model.

📝 Plan

What are your steps? Use your model to guide your plan.

_____

_____

_____

🛠️ Create

Follow your plan. What is working? Do you need to try something else?

_____

_____

🔄 Improve

How could you make it better?

_____

_____

💬 Communicate

How well did it work? Is the problem solved?

_____

_____

☀️ Reflect

How did the placement of the flashlight affect the length of the shadow?

_____

_____

_____

Name _____

Read the task. Then, follow the steps to complete the task.

Breakfast Is for the Birds

Create a bird feeder that is protected from rain.

Materials

cardboard milk carton	scissors
glue or masking tape	string
hole punch	toothpicks or wooden craft sticks
paper towel tubes	birdseed

 Ask

What do you know? What do you need to know to get started?

_____

_____

Imagine

What could you do?

_____

_____

Plan

Choose an idea. Draw a model.

📝 Plan

What are your steps? Use your model to guide your plan.

_____

_____

_____

🔧 Create

Follow your plan. What is working? Do you need to try something else?

_____

_____

🔄 Improve

How could you make it better?

_____

_____

💬 Communicate

How well did it work? Is the problem solved?

_____

_____

☀️ Reflect

What other materials would make a more waterproof bird feeder?

_____

_____

_____

Name _____

Read the task. Then, follow the steps to complete the task.

Soil Inspection: Plants

Find the best type of soil to grow beans in.

Materials

bean seeds
cups
a variety of soils,
    such as ones that
    are sandy, silty, and
    high in clay

ruler, meterstick, or
    measuring tape
water
window that receives
    sunlight

Caution: Before beginning any nature activity, ask families' permission and inquire about students' plant allergies. Remind students not to touch potentially harmful plants during the activity.

🔲 Ask

What do you know? What do you need to know to get started?

_____

_____

☁ Imagine

What could you do?

_____

_____

📝 Plan

Choose an idea. Draw a model.

📓 Plan

What are your steps? Use your model to guide your plan.

_____

_____

_____

🛠 Create

Follow your plan. What is working? Do you need to try something else?

_____

_____

🔄 Improve

How could you make it better?

_____

_____

💬 Communicate

How well did it work? Is the problem solved?

_____

_____

☀ Reflect

What are some words that describe the soil that worked best?

_____

_____

_____

Name _____

Read the task. Then, follow the steps to complete the task.

Simply Marble-ous: Gravity

Create a path along a wall that will make a marble take more than 20 seconds to reach the bottom.

Materials

marbles	timer
masking tape	wall (or a solid
paper towel tubes	surface, such as a
scissors	piece of cardboard)

Ask

What do you know? What do you need to know to get started?

_____

_____

Imagine

What could you do?

_____

_____

Plan

Choose an idea. Draw a model.

📝 Plan

What are your steps? Use your model to guide your plan.

_____

_____

_____

🔧 Create

Follow your plan. What is working? Do you need to try something else?

_____

_____

🔄 Improve

How could you make it better?

_____

_____

💬 Communicate

How well did it work? Is the problem solved?

_____

_____

☀ Reflect

What helped slow down the marble?

_____

_____

_____

Name _____

Read the task. Then, follow the steps to complete the task.

Make Your Own Play Dough: Chemistry

Create play dough that can be rolled into a ball and hold a shape.

Materials

flour	measuring cups
salt	measuring spoons
water	newspaper
food coloring	spoon
large mixing bowl	

Caution: Before beginning any food activity, ask families' permission and inquire about students' food allergies and religious or other restrictions.

🅿 Ask

What do you know? What do you need to know to get started?

_____

_____

💭 Imagine

What could you do?

_____

_____

📓 Plan

Choose an idea. Draw a model.

📓 Plan

What are your steps? Use your model to guide your plan.

_____

_____

_____

🛠 Create

Follow your plan. What is working? Do you need to try something else?

_____

_____

🔄 Improve

How could you make it better?

_____

_____

💬 Communicate

How well did it work? Is the problem solved?

_____

_____

🌟 Reflect

What recipe would you write for others to make play dough?

_____

_____

_____

Name _____

Read the task. Then, follow the steps to complete the task.

Box Banjo: Sound

Create a banjo that can play different notes.

Materials

rubber bands in different sizes and widths

string or yarn

a variety of empty boxes, such as tissue boxes, check boxes, or shoe boxes

Ask

What do you know? What do you need to know to get started?

_____

_____

Imagine

What could you do?

_____

_____

Plan

Choose an idea. Draw a model.

📝 Plan

What are your steps? Use your model to guide your plan.

_____

_____

_____

🛠 Create

Follow your plan. What is working? Do you need to try something else?

_____

_____

🔄 Improve

How could you make it better?

_____

_____

💬 Communicate

How well did it work? Is the problem solved?

_____

_____

☀ Reflect

Are all of the strings on a real banjo or guitar the same? If not, what is different about the strings?

_____

_____

_____

Name _____

Read the task. Then, follow the steps to complete the task.

Rain Collector: Weather

Create a device to collect and measure rainwater.

Materials

empty plastic bottles   ruler
   and containers   meterstick
markers   string

Ask

What do you know? What do you need to know to get started?

_____

_____

Imagine

What could you do?

_____

_____

Plan

Choose an idea. Draw a model.

📝 Plan

What are your steps? Use your model to guide your plan.

_____

_____

_____

⚒️ Create

Follow your plan. What is working? Do you need to try something else?

_____

_____

🔄 Improve

How could you make it better?

_____

_____

💬 Communicate

How well did it work? Is the problem solved?

_____

_____

☀️ Reflect

If others made rain collectors, would they get the same results? Why or why not?

_____

_____

_____

Name _____

Read the task. Then, follow the steps to complete the task.

The Mad Hatter

Create a hat that can hold a sheet of paper in front of you.

Materials

You may use any items you choose, such as fabric, cardboard, construction paper, and newspaper.

glue
scissors
stapler
tape

Ask

What do you know? What do you need to know to get started?

_____

_____

Imagine

What could you do?

_____

_____

Plan

Choose an idea. Draw a model.

📓 Plan

What are your steps? Use your model to guide your plan.

_____

_____

_____

🛠️ Create

Follow your plan. What is working? Do you need to try something else?

_____

_____

🔄 Improve

How could you make it better?

_____

_____

💬 Communicate

How well did it work? Is the problem solved?

_____

_____

☀️ Reflect

What was the hardest part of making the hat work?

_____

_____

_____

Name _____

Read the task. Then, follow the steps to complete the task.

It's Not Easy Making Green

Use two or more different colors of paint to create at least three different shades of green.

Materials

bowls or plates for
  paint
newspaper
paintbrushes

paper
washable paint in a
  variety of colors

Ask

What do you know? What do you need to know to get started?

_____

_____

Imagine

What could you do?

_____

_____

Plan

Choose an idea. Draw a model.

📓 Plan

What are your steps? Use your model to guide your plan.

_____

_____

_____

🛠 Create

Follow your plan. What is working? Do you need to try something else?

_____

_____

🔄 Improve

How could you make it better?

_____

_____

💬 Communicate

How well did it work? Is the problem solved?

_____

_____

☀ Reflect

How would you make a lighter shade of green? A darker shade of green?

_____

_____

_____

Name _____

Read the task. Then, follow the steps to complete the task.

House of Cards

Without using glue or tape, create a card house that is at least 1 foot (30 cm) tall.

Materials

ruler or meterstick   playing cards

🅱 Ask

What do you know? What do you need to know to get started?

_____

_____

☁ Imagine

What could you do?

_____

_____

📝 Plan

Choose an idea. Draw a model.

📓 Plan

What are your steps? Use your model to guide your plan.

_____

_____

_____

🛠 Create

Follow your plan. What is working? Do you need to try something else?

_____

_____

🔄 Improve

How could you make it better?

_____

_____

💬 Communicate

How well did it work? Is the problem solved?

_____

_____

☀ Reflect

What are some reasons why your card house might fall?

_____

_____

_____

Name _____

Read the task. Then, follow the steps to complete the task.

The Domino Effect: Physics

Line up dominoes so that, when they fall, they cause something else to roll or fall.

Materials

dominoes
flat surface

small rolling object,
such as a toy car,
marble, or ball

Ask

What do you know? What do you need to know to get started?

_____

_____

Imagine

What could you do?

_____

_____

Plan

Choose an idea. Draw a model.

Plan

What are your steps? Use your model to guide your plan.

_____

_____

_____

_____

Create

Follow your plan. What is working? Do you need to try something else?

_____

_____

Improve

How could you make it better?

_____

_____

Communicate

How well did it work? Is the problem solved?

_____

_____

Reflect

What other tricks could you do with the dominoes?

_____

_____

_____

Name _____

Read the task. Then, follow the steps to complete the task.

Float That Boat!

Create a boat that floats.

Materials

You may use any items you choose, such as clay, aluminum foil, toothpicks, or newspaper.

container of water
glue
scissors
tape

Ask

What do you know? What do you need to know to get started?

_____

_____

Imagine

What could you do?

_____

_____

Plan

Choose an idea. Draw a model.

📓 Plan

What are your steps? Use your model to guide your plan.

_____

_____

_____

🛠️ Create

Follow your plan. What is working? Do you need to try something else?

_____

_____

🔄 Improve

How could you make it better?

_____

_____

💬 Communicate

How well did it work? Is the problem solved?

_____

_____

☀️ Reflect

What other supplies would you use if you wanted to make a larger boat?

_____

_____

_____

Name _____

Read the task. Then, follow the steps to complete the task.

Marshmallow Mansion

Create the tallest structure you can. It must be able to stand on its own.

Materials

flat surface
miniature
   marshmallows

wooden toothpicks

Caution: Before beginning any food activity, ask families' permission and inquire about students' food allergies and religious or other restrictions.

Ask

What do you know? What do you need to know to get started?

_____

_____

Imagine

What could you do?

_____

_____

Plan

Choose an idea. Draw a model.

Plan

What are your steps? Use your model to guide your plan.

_____

_____

_____

Create

Follow your plan. What is working? Do you need to try something else?

_____

Improve

How could you make it better?

_____

Communicate

How well did it work? Is the problem solved?

_____

Reflect

What is the difference between the bottom of your structure and the top?

_____

_____

Name _____

Read the task. Then, follow the steps to complete the task.

Big Bubble Blast

Create the largest bubble you can.

Materials

bubble solution   pans, such as pie
chenille stems   or roasting pans
string or yarn   ruler or meterstick

Ask

What do you know? What do you need to know to get started?

_____

_____

Imagine

What could you do?

_____

_____

Plan

Choose an idea. Draw a model.

📝 Plan

What are your steps? Use your model to guide your plan.

_____

_____

_____

🛠 Create

Follow your plan. What is working? Do you need to try something else?

_____

_____

🔄 Improve

How could you make it better?

_____

_____

💬 Communicate

How well did it work? Is the problem solved?

_____

_____

🔆 Reflect

What other supplies do you think you would need to make even larger bubbles?

_____

_____

_____

Name _____

Read the task. Then, follow the steps to complete the task.

Hide That Sound!

Find a way to soften the sound of a noisy toy.

Materials

plastic or cardboard boxes	newspaper
cotton balls	noisy toy, such as an egg shaker or a
felt	jingle bell

✋ Ask

What do you know? What do you need to know to get started?

_____

_____

💭 Imagine

What could you do?

_____

_____

📝 Plan

Choose an idea. Draw a model.

📓 Plan

What are your steps? Use your model to guide your plan.

_____

_____

_____

🛠 Create

Follow your plan. What is working? Do you need to try something else?

_____

_____

🔄 Improve

How could you make it better?

_____

_____

💬 Communicate

How well did it work? Is the problem solved?

_____

_____

🔆 Reflect

How could this information help you in real life?

_____

_____

_____

Name _____

Read the task. Then, follow the steps to complete the task.

No Place Like Home: Habitats

Create a home for a small animal of your choice.

Materials

You may use any items you choose, such as cardboard tubes, grass, rocks, and water.

empty container, such as a shoe box or a small, empty, plastic aquarium

---

🔲 Ask

What do you know? What do you need to know to get started?

_____

_____

💭 Imagine

What could you do?

_____

_____

📝 Plan

Choose an idea. Draw a model.

📝 Plan

What are your steps? Use your model to guide your plan.

_____

_____

_____

🛠 Create

Follow your plan. What is working? Do you need to try something else?

_____

_____

🔄 Improve

How could you make it better?

_____

_____

💬 Communicate

How well did it work? Is the problem solved?

_____

_____

☀ Reflect

What other animals would survive in the home you created? What animals would not survive there?

_____

_____

_____

Name _____

Read the task. Then, follow the steps to complete the task.

Soaring Sock

Create a wind sock that will fly in the wind.

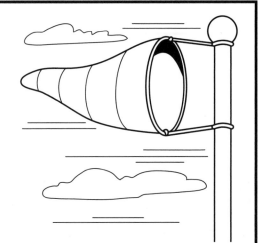

Materials

chenille stems	fabric
wooden craft sticks	ribbons
crepe paper	glue
tissue paper	scissors
newspaper	stapler
construction paper	tape

 Ask

What do you know? What do you need to know to get started?

_____

_____

Imagine

What could you do?

_____

_____

Plan

Choose an idea. Draw a model.

Plan

What are your steps? Use your model to guide your plan.

_____

_____

_____

Create

Follow your plan. What is working? Do you need to try something else?

_____

_____

Improve

How could you make it better?

_____

_____

Communicate

How well did it work? Is the problem solved?

_____

_____

Reflect

What helped your wind sock fly?

_____

_____

_____

Name _____

Read the task. Then, follow the steps to complete the task.

Road Work: Friction

Create a ramp that will cause a toy car to gain speed going down it.

Materials

toy car	cellophane
carpet scraps	sandpaper
plastic	glue
paper	tape
fabric	scissors
wax paper	timer

Ask

What do you know? What do you need to know to get started?

_____

_____

Imagine

What could you do?

_____

_____

Plan

Choose an idea. Draw a model.

📓 Plan

What are your steps? Use your model to guide your plan.

_____

_____

_____

🛠 Create

Follow your plan. What is working? Do you need to try something else?

_____

_____

🔄 Improve

How could you make it better?

_____

_____

💬 Communicate

How well did it work? Is the problem solved?

_____

_____

☀ Reflect

What materials slowed down the toy car? Why?

_____

_____

_____

Name _____

Read the task. Then, follow the steps to complete the task.

A to Xylophone

Create a working xylophone.

Materials

dowel or stick
  (to be used as a
  mallet)
empty box or
  container
glue
tape

a variety of metal,
  wood, and
  plastic materials,
  such as metal
  spoons or
  wooden craft
  sticks

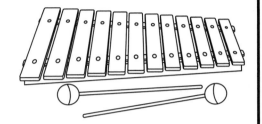

Ask

What do you know? What do you need to know to get started?

_____

_____

Imagine

What could you do?

_____

_____

Plan

Choose an idea. Draw a model.

📓 Plan

What are your steps? Use your model to guide your plan.

_____

_____

_____

🛠️ Create

Follow your plan. What is working? Do you need to try something else?

_____

_____

🔄 Improve

How could you make it better?

_____

_____

💬 Communicate

How well did it work? Is the problem solved?

_____

_____

☀️ Reflect

Which materials made the loudest sounds?

_____

_____

_____

Name _____

Read the task. Then, follow the steps to complete the task.

Picky Ants: Animal Behavior

Find what food ants like best so that people will avoid bringing it on picnics. This is an outdoor activity!

Materials

paper
paper plates
pencil

a variety of foods,
    such as fruit,
    cookies, and
    margarine

Caution: Before beginning any food activity, ask families' permission and inquire about students' food allergies and religious or other restrictions.

🔑 Ask

What do you know? What do you need to know to get started?

_____

_____

💭 Imagine

What could you do?

_____

_____

📝 Plan

Choose an idea. Draw a model.

📝 Plan

What are your steps? Use your model to guide your plan.

_____

_____

_____

🛠️ Create

Follow your plan. What is working? Do you need to try something else?

_____

_____

🔄 Improve

How could you make it better?

_____

_____

💬 Communicate

How well did it work? Is the problem solved?

_____

_____

☀️ Reflect

How did you know that the ants liked certain foods better than others?

_____

_____

_____

Name _____

Read the task. Then, follow the steps to complete the task.

Sun Scientist: Earth Science

Prove that the sun's rays heat the earth by melting something outside.

Materials

You may use any items you choose, such as
   aluminum foil and construction paper.

small containers, such as
   cardboard boxes or paper bowls
items that melt easily, such as
   crayons or ice cubes

 Ask

What do you know? What do you need to know to get started?

_____

_____

 Imagine

What could you do?

_____

_____

Plan

Choose an idea. Draw a model.

📝 Plan

What are your steps? Use your model to guide your plan.

_____

_____

_____

🔧 Create

Follow your plan. What is working? Do you need to try something else?

_____

_____

🔄 Improve

How could you make it better?

_____

_____

💬 Communicate

How well did it work? Is the problem solved?

_____

_____

☀ Reflect

Where would your creation work? Where would it not work?

_____

_____

_____

Name _____

Read the task. Then, follow the steps to complete the task.

Pop-Up Paper

Create a pop-up greeting card.

Materials

construction paper	pencil
crayons or markers	scissors
glue	tape

Ask

What do you know? What do you need to know to get started?

_____

_____

Imagine

What could you do?

_____

_____

Plan

Choose an idea. Draw a model.

📝 Plan

What are your steps? Use your model to guide your plan.

_____

_____

_____

✂️ Create

Follow your plan. What is working? Do you need to try something else?

_____

_____

🔄 Improve

How could you make it better?

_____

_____

💬 Communicate

How well did it work? Is the problem solved?

_____

_____

🌟 Reflect

Explain a trick for making a particular shape pop up.

_____

_____

_____

Name _____

Read the task. Then, follow the steps to complete the task.

An A-peel-ing Banana

Find a way to keep a peeled banana slice from turning brown.

Materials

peeled banana slices	apple juice
plates	lemon juice
aluminum foil	orange juice
cellophane	milk
wax paper	water

Caution: Before beginning any food activity, ask families' permission and inquire about students' food allergies and religious or other restrictions.

 Ask

What do you know? What do you need to know to get started?

_____

_____

Imagine

What could you do?

_____

_____

Plan

Choose an idea. Draw a model.

📝 Plan

What are your steps? Use your model to guide your plan.

_____

_____

_____

🔧 Create

Follow your plan. What is working? Do you need to try something else?

_____

_____

🔄 Improve

How could you make it better?

_____

_____

💬 Communicate

How well did it work? Is the problem solved?

_____

_____

☀ Reflect

How could this information be helpful for other foods?

_____

_____

_____

Name _____

Read the task. Then, follow the steps to complete the task.

Game On!

Use an empty egg carton to create a game.

Materials

You may use any items you choose, such as
   cotton balls, dice, linking cubes, or marbles.

empty egg carton
construction paper
wooden craft sticks
chenille stems
markers or crayons
pencil

Ask

What do you know? What do you need to know to get started?

_____

_____

Imagine

What could you do?

_____

_____

Plan

Choose an idea. Draw a model.

📝 Plan

What are your steps? Use your model to guide your plan.

_____

_____

_____

🛠 Create

Follow your plan. What is working? Do you need to try something else?

_____

_____

🔄 Improve

How could you make it better?

_____

_____

💬 Communicate

How well did it work? Is the problem solved?

_____

_____

☀ Reflect

What are the rules of your game? How does a player win?

_____

_____

_____

Name _____

Read the task. Then, follow the steps to complete the task.

Can You Hear Me?

Create a device that will allow you to hear a friend from across the room.

Materials

You may use any items you choose, such as cardboard tubes, disposable foam cups, or paper cups.

string or yarn
pencil with a sharp point
paper
scissors
tape
glue

 Ask

What do you know? What do you need to know to get started?

_____

_____

 Imagine

What could you do?

_____

_____

Plan

Choose an idea. Draw a model.

📓 Plan

What are your steps? Use your model to guide your plan.

_____

_____

_____

🛠 Create

Follow your plan. What is working? Do you need to try something else?

_____

_____

🔄 Improve

How could you make it better?

_____

_____

💬 Communicate

How well did it work? Is the problem solved?

_____

_____

☀ Reflect

What supplies did not work? Why?

_____

_____

_____

Name _____

Read the task. Then, follow the steps to complete the task.

Soil-Free Seeds: Plants

Grow bean plants without soil.

Materials

bean seeds   plastic bags
cotton balls   paper towels
disposable foam cups   water
  or paper cups

Caution: Plastic bags present a suffocation hazard. Keep bags away from babies and small children.

Ask

What do you know? What do you need to know to get started?

_____

_____

Imagine

What could you do?

_____

_____

Plan

Choose an idea. Draw a model.

Plan

What are your steps? Use your model to guide your plan.

_____

_____

_____

Create

Follow your plan. What is working? Do you need to try something else?

_____

_____

Improve

How could you make it better?

_____

_____

Communicate

How well did it work? Is the problem solved?

_____

_____

Reflect

Think about how you were able to grow your bean plant without soil. What purpose did your supplies serve that soil normally would help with?

_____

_____

 © Carson-Dellosa · CD-104852 · Applying the Standards: STEM

Name _____

Read the task. Then, follow the steps to complete the task.

Cairn Creation

A *cairn* is a pile of rocks that are stacked as a landmark. Use rocks to create the highest tower you can.

Materials

flat surface
rocks (in a variety of
   shapes and sizes)

meterstick
ruler

Ask

What do you know? What do you need to know to get started?

_____

_____

Imagine

What could you do?

_____

_____

Plan

Choose an idea. Draw a model.

📝 Plan

What are your steps? Use your model to guide your plan.

_____

_____

_____

🛠 Create

Follow your plan. What is working? Do you need to try something else?

_____

_____

🔄 Improve

How could you make it better?

_____

_____

💬 Communicate

How well did it work? Is the problem solved?

_____

_____

☀ Reflect

What are some tips you would give others for how to create a rock tower?

_____

_____

_____

© Carson-Dellosa · CD-104852 · Applying the Standards: STEM

Name _____

Read the task. Then, follow the steps to complete the task.

Repurposing with a Purpose: Environmental Awareness

To repurpose means to reuse something for a different purpose. Use recyclables to create a new toy.

Materials

You may use any items you choose, such as
   cardboard boxes,
   plastic bottles
   and containers,
   or egg and milk
   cartons.
string or yarn

markers or crayons
construction paper
ribbons
paper
scissors
stapler
tape
glue

 Ask

What do you know? What do you need to know to get started?

_____

_____

Imagine

What could you do?

_____

_____

Plan

Choose an idea. Draw a model.

📓 Plan

What are your steps? Use your model to guide your plan.

_____

_____

_____

⚒️ Create

Follow your plan. What is working? Do you need to try something else?

_____

_____

🔄 Improve

How could you make it better?

_____

_____

💬 Communicate

How well did it work? Is the problem solved?

_____

_____

☀️ Reflect

What are some other things that can be repurposed?

_____

_____

_____